Can You Please Explain That?

A Course in Miracles in real life applications and plain English

By Kristine Jo Stout

For Leanne

Foreword

When I first picked up *A Course in Miracles* in January of 2019, I couldn't make heads or tails of it! Knowing absolutely nothing about it, I of course started on page one, with every intention of reading the entire book. But it took me two weeks to get through Chapter One! I was sure reading a mechanical manual daily would be just as exciting, and just as confusing. So taking some advice from a Facebook Group, I switched up and started doing the daily lessons instead. Things got a bit easier. Then engaging with others who've read the book, and by attending a few retreats, things got even better. My understanding was also enhanced by numerous other spiritual texts and leaders that kept showing up for me to read and study, reinforcing my understanding of the Course. But it wasn't until I met a young woman online, who reached out to me for help through this Facebook Group, that I started really applying what I read in those pages, and then understanding grew exponentially. She was in a terrible place mentally and physically, and she asked me all kinds of spiritually complicated questions about ACIM and life in general, and to my surprise, the answers to her questions just appeared on the screen in front of me! I can't tell you how many times I looked back over what I had written to her and flat out marveled at the words on the page, asking myself in a kind of awe, "Where did that come from?" I believe the Holy Spirit guided my advice and answers to her questions. I wrote this booklet from those conversations, knitting those answers into a (hopefully) congruous flow that you will find both inspirational and instructive. I followed this text from *A Course in Miracles* when talking with Leanne, and while putting this book together:

I am here only to be truly helpful.

I am here to represent Him Who sent me.

I do not have to worry about what to say or what to do, because He Who sent me will direct me.

I am content to be wherever He wishes, knowing He goes there with me.

I will be healed as I let Him teach me to heal.

--A Course in Miracles, text Chapter 2, section 18

At time of printing, this young woman is doing so much better, and I'm so proud of her! She is no longer self-harming, and has become mentally and physically stronger, a little at a time. I have truly witnessed a miracle!

Copyright © 2023 Kristine Jo Stout

All rights reserved. No part of this book may be reproduced or used in any manner without the prior written permission of the copyright owner, except for the use of brief quotations in a book review.

To request permissions, contact the publisher at info@amazon-publications.com

Paperback: 978-1-960657-09-1

Edited by **Kristine Jo Stout**
Cover art by **Amazon Publications**
Layout by **Kristine Jo Stout**

Amazon Publications Group
832 BROADWAY NEW YORK NY 10003-4817 USA

Amazon-publications.com

+1 (646)-458-4222

Table of Contents

Chapter 1 8
   Who is God? Who am I? 8
   Metaphors 9
   Growth 10

Chapter 2 12
   The World of Separation 12
   Ego and the Game 12
   Time 15
   The Dream 17
   The Mirror 19
   In the World but not Of the World 20
   Forgiveness 21

Chapter 3 22
   Love More, Fear Less. 22
   Attachments 23

Chapter 4 25
   Which Teacher 25

The Voice in your Head 25
  The Tiny Mad Idea 27
  Hard Times 30

Chapter 5 32
  Thoughts and Beliefs 32
  The Leaky Roof 32
  Seeing 33
  Is it Really Real? 37
  Guilt 40

Chapter 6 43
  The Bible 43

Chapter 7 45
  Attitude 45
  Health 48
  "BROKEN" 49
  Good and Bad 51
  Practical Advice 52
  Addiction and Meditation 55
  Caring 56

Chapter 8 58
    Fear 58

Acknowledgements 61

About the Author 62
    Kristine offers free Life Coaching! Get in touch with her today. 62

Chapter 1

Who is God? Who am I?

How do you describe the indescribable? How do you put the infinite into finite words?

The answer is Love, as you might expect, but not the "love" you might expect. Spirit is pure Unconditional Love, and humans really don't understand just what that means. Love on earth is a verb—something you do. But Unconditional Love is a noun--something that Is. It is existence itself. It is peace and bliss. It is pure consciousness. Pure awareness. It is the Creator. It is your Right Mind. It just Is. God's "name" is "I Am". It is all that is, and therefore is *in* all there is, including in You.

If you wish to know Spirit, God, The Right Mind, The Teacher of Peace, The Holy Spirit, you can't learn about it. You need to connect to it to experience it. You do that by aligning your *thoughts* with its thoughts. Spirit is joy, peace, kindness, bliss, love. If your *thoughts* are of these things, the feeling in your heart you are experiencing is Spirit, and you recognize your Oneness with It in that moment. If your thoughts are aligned with sadness, regret, misery, grief, disease, confusion, separation, your thoughts are aligned with Ego, The Wrong Mind, The False Self, The Teacher of Chaos, The Separate Self. Then you are about as far from Spirit that you can take yourself. But the good news is that your thoughts are a product of what you believe, and you can *change your mind* (challenge your beliefs)! Any time, any place, and in any circumstance!

Metaphors

Metaphors are an ingenious little trick we can use to understand the un-understandable. These will give you a rough idea of what Oneness is *like*. We are all connected, and we are all part of God. What one does has an effect on the whole. Our very existence is that of being One with God. At Home with Him is where our happiness (our treasure) is. We are aspects of God himself—sent out into 3D to explore and learn and feel and be and find our way back.

Imagine a white sand beach stretching on and on as far as you can see. The beach is God and we are grains of sand.

Imagine the earth's beautiful oceans. God is the ocean and we are droplets of water.

God is the body and we are the individual cells of that body.

Imagine the universe and all its infinite beauty. God is the universe and we are the planets and stars.

Imagine a beautiful diamond—big as a star. God is the diamond and we are the facets, or faces on the diamond.

If God is a symphony, we are the music notes.

If God is a portrait, we are the paint.

Growth

One of the aspects of God is Growth. You can even see it here on the earth: babies grow into adults, seeds grow into plants and give us food and flowers, acorns grow into trees. The Way of God is growth. He even provides a means of nurturing us all here to be sure we have what we need to grow. And humans are meant to grow physically, mentally, and spiritually.

This answered a good many questions for me once I realized this. I often wondered why, if we were already perfect, in harmony and oneness with God, would we ever leave that state? What good does it do us or anyone to come here and experience separateness, and in that, experience such horrendous pain and suffering? What's the point? And Growth is the answer. I wondered how perfection could improve on itself, too. And it came to me with this realization about growth: Examine an acorn. It is perfect exactly how it is. Within it is contained the blueprint of a mighty oak tree that will tower in the sky and rain down thousands of acorns of its own in its lifetime. I think we are like that acorn. We are perfect just as we are, and at the same time, we have such incredible potential! How does the acorn turn into the mighty oak tree? Growth is a mystery even to modern day scientists. That's because it's a miracle, and science hasn't quite figured those out. We agreed to come here because we knew that if we did, we could become an oak tree. Why would we decide to stay an acorn?

Nature isn't encumbered by Ego. Watch a garden sprout and grow. Watch an incredible oak tree spring up from a tiny acorn. Watch a caterpillar transform into a butterfly. Watch an egg hatch and a baby bird grow and learn to fly. Growth is an amazing transformation, a natural extension of the Love of God.

Chapter 2

The World of Separation

Ego and the Game

The first thing you need to realize is that it is impossible to ever be separate from God. In Truth we are all God heads, infinite, immortal, omniscient Beings just like our Father.

The second thing you need to realize is that life is a game. And not just any game. It's a Game played by infinite, immortal, omniscient Beings. So the question is, how do you fool a Being like that into thinking he could ever be separate from the Father? You can't play the Separation Game unless you *forget*. Forget your Oneness with God. Forget your true nature. Forget about your rightful inheritance. Oh, all that is still true. You've only forgotten.

The Ego was provided as a tool to help conceal Oneness. It makes the *belief* in separation possible. Among its many functions, it gave humans a sense of privacy, and sense of individuality. And it gave us a way to know when we're in danger, a tool of protection. It's a necessary part of life on earth. It was provided for us by God along with the earth, sky, moon, animals, oceans, planets, and everything else. It's a system. Like gravity. It has a purpose. Gravity's purpose is to keep objects from floating off into outer space. The Ego's purpose is to help us forget we are One with God. The Ego is not inherently evil. The problem came from the Ego taking over our identity. Most of us, if you ask who they are, will tell you they're a man, woman, doctor, redhead, artist, housewife, etc. These are all Ego identities. These are not who you are. Not even close.

Over the centuries the Ego has morphed into something it was never meant to be, and it has become too powerful, fear's grip too tight for most of us. It has done its job too well, and we are having an extremely difficult time dis-identifying with it and remembering our true self. This separation "reality" is too convincing for us to think it's only illusion. That's why writings like *A Course in Miracles* came into being.

But God knows we're mistaken, He knows we are not our Ego, and doesn't leave us here alone. Spirit made it possible to see through this illusion. How? Just look with your heart, not your eyes. Remember *A Course in Miracles*: "Above all else, I want to see."[1] It is this heart-sight that can see past the Ego, past the mask of separation that we wear. It demonstrates the truth: that there was never any separation, because that's impossible. Remember this, see the Truth in yourself and your brothers, and you win the Game.

Of course if it was easy, it wouldn't be much of a game. You see, you have been programmed to think you are separate from God, and that there are terrible, fearful things all around you. If you only operate within the parameters of your programming, you see terrible, fearful things around you all the time, and you live your life within this context. In fact, the Ego is most happy to

---

[1] *A Course in Miracles* Lesson 27

arrange to show all kinds of fearful forms off to you, one by one. Most of us throughout the centuries have lived this, and only this kind of existence.

But you were also given direct access to the Holy Spirit, who sees you for the One Christ Mind that you are in Truth. The object of the Game is to find the Holy Spirit and Oneness within by overcoming and quieting your fearful Egoic programming, laying it aside, and following the Holy Spirit's voice instead. In other words, the object of the game is to create miracles. You have a built-in guidance system to help you know which Mind is speaking at any given time: if something creates the feeling of fear in you, it is of the Ego. If something creates the feeling of joy within you, it's of the Holy Spirit. But the Ego is noisy and the Holy Spirit is quiet. The Ego is hard to ignore, and the Holy Spirit is subtle and harder to hear. The Ego is of the mind, the Holy Spirit is of the heart. It's an extremely difficult game and only the very bravest souls volunteer to play. You are in Truth, one of those souls.

So did God send us here? No, He didn't exactly choose to send us here. We are part of Him—equals—and He doesn't order us around like servants. It's more like He asked for volunteers to go and check out this impossible world of separation first hand, and we jumped at the chance to do it. We were very excited about it! What an incredible opportunity! What an incredible challenge! Everything was laid out for us—the idea of the world and the universe, the animals and plants, the land and sky and ocean, the Ego, pain, sorrow, evil, all of it. We knew exactly what we were taking on, and we came here joyfully. The Ego was given to us to help us *believe* in separation. You must understand we are infinite, omniscient God-heads. It's not easy to trick us into believing something as absurd as the idea of Separation from God. The Ego was put in place to help us really believe it, and it's certainly sly and crafty enough to do its job. Because if we came here remembering who we really were, we couldn't experience Separation at all, and the whole earth experiment would be ruined. So, take comfort in this: we never left His side. It just seems like we did.

So now the challenge is to find our way out of forgetfulness and back to our Source—out of fear, back to Love (Self). In doing this we grow. Trusting God is essential to finding your Self. Ego fights with God, wanting to be separate. But it wants what can never be. Trust, go with the flow, let go and let God, walk the straight and narrow path, whatever you want to call it. Don't worry about the reasons why he leads you the way he does. He knows the destination, and you don't.

Time

You already know we have the past, the present, and the future that makes up our idea of time. The past is easy enough to understand, being something we've already experienced. Once something is in the past, it becomes a memory. A memory is just a bunch of images (illusions) and thoughts in your mind. Memories, the past, are just thought forms. They often have very little truth in them, because what you remember is tainted by your viewpoint. The future is more of a mystery, but it comes down to the same thing. It's not real, either. It's a bunch of thought forms, though it's made of worry, speculation, anticipation, excitement, dread—and all sorts of different things that haven't even happened yet, and may never come to pass. They're different than thoughts from the past, but still thoughts. But the present, the Now, is altogether different. It unfolds continually. Think of it like this: time is like a line. There is a point on the line called Now, and it travels forward along the line. Behind it is the past. In front is the future. The line itself is not real, but the point on the line is. Now is when everything happens. No exceptions. Now is eternal. Eternal means Real. That's how you can come to remember what is real: it's eternal. Spirit is eternal. Spirit is real. That's why if you stay in the Now instead of brooding on the past or worrying about the future, you're thoughts are aligned with the eternal. With Now. With Spirit. Past and future thoughts are illusions and memories. They're not real, being conjured by the Ego.

Confused yet? The Ego seems to be something totally opposite of God, so why would He create it? The answer is, it's not a true creation, any more than the earth or our bodies are true creations. It's all part of this illusionary system. Remember, it is impossible for you or I to actually be separate from God. But we can be tricked into believing we are. That's what we signed up for when we decided to come to this earth: amnesia. And we are having the separation experience for God *as God*. We're providing him with first-hand knowledge of what it feels like to believe we're separated from Him.

The answer is also, Love (God) has no opposite. There is nothing in Truth that is the opposite of God. Everything in this world is either Love, or a call for Love. We just have a hard time seeing it because of our amnesia. But amnesia is in your head. God dwells in your heart. Love is not of the head, it's of the heart.

Also, we never made a choice to leave God. It's actually not a thing. It's impossible to leave God. We only agreed to temporarily forget so we could participate in this earth experiment. You should know that only the brightest stars, only the bravest souls come here. It's even possible that our growth here may prepare us to pass God Himself in power. That's every teacher's hope for their students—that they grow beyond their teaching into something greater than they are. You have no idea who you are. You are truly astounding—a bright eternal soul worthy of…who knows what's in store for you? Just know, what you're working toward here will be eternal. Your "reward" will be *real*. What you're experiencing here under the influence of the Ego is only temporary. Pain and sorrow and confusion are only temporary.

A Course in Miracles states in its opening paragraphs, "Nothing real can be threatened, nothing unreal exists. Herein lies the peace of God."[2] Pain and sorrow and confusion and the Ego are unreal. Your eternal soul is real.

The Dream

Many spiritual teachers describe the earth experience as being a dream. They will say, "You are not the figure in

---

[2] *A Course in Miracles* Preface page x

the dream. You are the dreamer of the dream." I never liked that way of looking at it because it makes it sound like our True Self is asleep somewhere and not the active participant in our lives it truly is. It also confuses you with the fact that you have actual dreams at night all the time, and the two are totally different from one another.

The dream idea is a metaphor—a parable. "Real" is a confusing word. It doesn't mean that nothing matters here just because nothing is real. It really just depends on your perspective. For you here living in this plane of existence, everything is convincingly, inarguably real. For your true self that is in direct communication with the Holy Spirit, the body and everything that happens to it is more like playing a virtual reality game. Or a dream. You are here now, and now is sacred, not meaningless, even if we don't understand the meaning. Cherish your time here, take care of yourself and your belongings. Be kind and loving as you navigate through the shifting tides of the fortunes of this world. Help others, be kind to them, too. Not because you feel a sense of duty, but because by living in love, you move closer to God's mind, and you learn to remember that all important connection with God. There you find your peace. The "You" who is your true self knows that whatever happens here, it will remain You, it will experience spiritual growth, and no harm will come to it. In that sense, nothing matters here. But for the "you" who is physically present here, it all matters. Very much. Your happiness and the happiness of everyone around you depends on it.

The Mirror

Another popular metaphor used by spiritual guides is the idea that the universe is a mirror. This is part of what is called "The Law of Attraction" or "The Law of Cause and Effect" idea propounded by Abraham Hicks. It means that whatever you believe, you're actually giving that to the universe (to God), and the universe mirrors it back to you in amazing, often unpredictable ways. If you are a happy, kind person, you're actually throwing happy, kind thoughts out into the universe, and the universe creates all kinds of happy, kind things just for you, to appear in your life. If you are a meek, sad, tormented person, you're actually throwing meek, sad, tormented thoughts out into the universe, and the universe creates all kinds of meek, sad, tormented things, just for you, to appear in your life. It's not quite as black and white as that, because we are complex creative creatures. Go and look up the vibrational chart that goes with this. The universe works on vibrational frequencies that correspond in manifestation to our emotions. The lowest vibration is the emotion of shame, and things like humiliation, self-harm, low self-esteem produce bucket loads of shame. That's what you're giving the universe, and the universe reflects that vibration right back to you. This is *not* punishment. This is just how things work. This is actually good news, and I'll tell you why: the highest frequency on the chart is love, and things like heart-felt service, kindness, and acts of love produce bucket loads of kindness and peace reflected back at you. And here's the most important part: your beliefs determine your thoughts, and your thoughts determine your emotions, and your emotions determine your vibration. If you are in a continual state of shame, what you do think will show up in your life? That's why we need to guard our thoughts very carefully, and be aware of the vibration we're sending out. This is part of the creation process. This is how we create our lives. This is how we mis-create—make things happen in our lives that we don't want. We send out low-frequency vibrations by our thoughts, feelings, and beliefs.

In the World but not Of the World

I'm sure you've heard this one before. But what does it really mean? It means the world is temporary. You can't find any lasting treasure here, because it all eventually fades, and is in truth, meaningless from an eternal (real) perspective. All things here eventually come to an end. But we are eternal beings. That's the truth of our existence. Our souls live forever—just like God. For we were created to be like him. Eternal beings are happy living in eternity, not in time. That's where our real treasure (happiness) is!

So if you attach yourself and your identity to those things that fade and decay, you are setting yourself up for disappointment. Investing in the Ego and obeying its commands may lead to worldly goods, but what good is that? You're now the owner of a whole bunch of illusion!

But if you stick like glue to thoughts of love and peace, you're preparing the way to Bliss. Investing your time and energy into learning to listen to The Holy Spirit leads you to your inheritance, which, as an heir to God, is real, true treasure.

Forgiveness

In short, you are Holy. I am Holy. We are Holy. We were created Holy and have never left this state. The belief in separation hides our holiness from us. If it didn't, we would remember our holiness, see right through the illusion of separateness, and no longer believe in the world. When *A Course in Miracles* says, "Above all else I want to see"[3] it means I want to see my holiness and my brother's holiness. I want to look past their Ego and see them for the Holy being they truly are. It takes forgiveness to "see" this way. Especially forgiveness for ever thinking we could possibly be separate from God.

It's really important to not think of God as one being and ourself as another, separate being. God didn't do anything *to* us. That's just not in His nature. It's also important to know how fortunate we are that we know this stuff! We live in a time when this knowledge is available to humans. It's really pretty amazing. My advice is to not spend too much time on the "why" and "how" of creation. Just Be in it. Life is a classroom, a game, a play, a story. Learn, but don't forget to lighten up and have some *fun*!

---

[3] *A Course in Miracles* Lesson 27

Chapter 3
Love More, Fear Less.

"I am not a body. I am free! For I am still as God created me!"[4] I am a shining star. I am a piece of infinity. I am made by God; made of the only thing He has to create with: Unconditional Love. I am love itself! Holy Spirit help me to remember who I am!"

Learn how to be kind to yourself, your inner child, and to others. Start by acknowledging that you are alive, and therefore valuable by default. God doesn't make junk. You are loved! You are worthy! You are an eternal divine being made of light and love.

You are pure love expressing and experiencing itself in human form. Your experiences here are priceless, and no one else could have them except you. Your job was to lose your Self, and you did an excellent job! Now your job is to find yourself again, and that leads you back to God, because your very nature is of God. You've only just forgotten. And there is no rush. Please don't think you have to hurry. Everyone, and I mean *everyone* finds their Self in God eventually. One way back is through pain. It's the hardest way, but you've already been through so much, you may be closer than you think.

Lighten up, be joyful, and don't take anything you see too seriously! The more you take it seriously, the more "real" it becomes for you. But you are love itself, not illusion! You are real. You are God.

---

[4] *A Course in Miracles* Lesson 199

Attachments

The Ego says attachments are necessary. It even goes so far as to say that if you're not attached like glue to someone, you don't truly care about them. Right? It says that if your entire life doesn't revolve around this person, then you don't really care enough about them, you don't deserve them, and you deserve to get dumped. Gaslighting at its finest! Nothing could be further from the truth!!

Example: let's say that a family member has "had enough" and leaves you. You were attached to this person because he was family, and part of your identity is defined by this relationship because of that attachment. So you feel hurt and abandoned. But the attachment itself is only part of your Ego identity—your false self.

So does this mean that you are better off not being attached to your family members? Yes! It does! Does that mean that you can't love them? No, it doesn't!! See, the attachment is not love. It's just a thing for putting limits on love: you can do *this* and I'll love you, but if you do *that*, I will stop loving you." That's what this family member demanded from you—*conditional* love. This is an important point: being unattached does *not* mean you are cruel or unloving. You can devote your life to someone and still be unattached to them, as long as you don't make your role into your *identity*. Being unattached means you are free. Being unattached says you won't lower your standards and accept anything less than God's Love.

Being unattached does not have to be scary. And being in a loving relationship doesn't have to be scary, either.

Keep in mind that absolutely nothing on this planet is permanent. People are born and die every day. But they don't die because of anything *you've* done. They die because it's part of the system. It's our way of exiting the earth. It has nothing to do with you. People form relationships and break up and leave each other all the time. In the example above, he left you because of *his* thoughts, not *yours*. It's true that you add certain energies to the relationship, and the truth is, sometimes those energies tend to push people away (the clingy fear of losing them being one example). But it's the thoughts of the person who's leaving that interprets those energies, determines if they will live with them or not, and decides whether to accept or reject them. Again, it's not up to you what other people decide to do. Nothing you can do will change their thoughts and beliefs. It has to come from within *them*.

So if it's temporary, it's not Unconditional Love. And all attachments here on this planet are temporary.

Chapter 4

Which Teacher

We have talked a lot about the Ego and the Holy Spirit, and how they both are available to you all the time. For this chapter we will think of them as teachers, and as part of our mind. The Ego is the Teacher of Chaos, or the Wrong Mind, and it operates within a system of the belief in separation. The Holy Spirit is the Teacher of Peace, or the Right Mind, and it operates within a system of knowledge of Oneness. There are only these two choices, and we switch back and forth between them all the time. But the Teacher of Chaos is our default. When you are distressed in any way, it's because you have been listening to his teachings. When you are at ease, loving and joyful, you have been listening to the Teacher of Peace. You know this because of the way you feel. Your emotions are your guidance system.

The Voice in your Head

The chatter in your head is loud and practically nonstop. It provides a continuous stream of commentary like what accompanies a football game. That chatter is all from the Teacher of Chaos. The voice of the Teacher of Peace is more like a *feeling* than a whisper; it's much quieter, but ever-present. It doesn't come from your head, it comes from your heart—your center. Intuition is a good example of the voice the Teacher of Peace. It's a prompting—a feeling—a sixth sense, and is behind the noise. It will guide your actions *if you choose to heed it*. You need a calm, quiet, still demeanor to even notice it, so if you're all upset, it's harder to notice. It's extremely easy to overlook it, rationalize it away, and discount it because it's so subtle, and we don't trust it. And the Teacher of Chaos shouts over it, and is loud, obnoxious, and speaks with its own brand of logic and authority. How many times have you had a feeling about something and you discounted it, did the opposite, and regretted it later? That's totally normal for humans. So it takes practice. Practice using the Right Mind to think with, practice watching out for that *feeling*, practice acknowledging, practice acting on it.

So if you're feeling terrible, stop and trace your emotions to their source. You'll find the Teacher of Chaos there, telling you how bad you are, or how worthless, stupid, afraid, insecure, ridiculous, or weak you are. Once you realize who's talking to you, you are free to tell it to shut up! Ask to speak with the Teacher of Peace, quiet your mind, and listen with your heart. Soon you'll *feel* it reminding you how loved you are, and how you've never been alone, and never will be.

The Teacher of Chaos is a liar. Of course, there are bits of truth in every lie, or it would just collapse. Learning not to take anything from this teacher too seriously is really important! Lighten up, smile, laugh even! The Teacher of Chaos hates that! Life is a game, and the rules Chaos gives you are quite ridiculous! Ultimately, everything you see and know around you is not what your senses tell you. Smile a little, laugh more, and worry not at all. Love is the only true reality, and it's in *everything*.

The Tiny Mad Idea

Once God had a tiny mad idea. He, being All There Is, wondered how it would feel to think He was separate from Himself. Crazy, right? What an incredibly delicious, crazy idea! At once the imagination of God sprang forth and manifested into a Big Bang and the idea of separation was born. But it was still only an idea. Everything created was still God and in God and made of God. We were created of the same thing the stars are made of, by the thoughts of God himself, and with His power of creation, too. But all these different aspects of God thought they were separate individuals! So far, the Tiny Mad Idea experiment was a success! This was done in part through use of the Ego, which gave us each a sense of separateness as well as a sense of privacy, and motivations to live, eat, prosper, take care and protect ourselves, etc. The Ego was just as "real" as the other creations. That is to say, none of it was real, because it was only temporary. Only eternal things are real.

But the Ego's role has now gotten totally out of hand, and we as a people think we are our Ego. We think we are this temporary body/mind, and we have forgotten our One True Nature. And now the Ego is trying to live forever, which is impossible because it's only a temporary construct! But it's very sly, crafty, and self-serving, and is terrified of the reality of Oneness, and of God. So now our creative power has been usurped by the Ego and of course, nasty, fearful, dark, and horrible manifestations come forth. This is what happens when we create using our Wrong Mind—The Ego—The Teacher of Chaos. In this dimension we have the power to hurt ourselves and others when we let this teacher do our thinking for us. None of it is actually happening from a higher perspective, but all of it seems perfectly real and solid here. Our creative power has the ability to create perpetrators and victims, sinners and saints, happiness or fear. If we create with our Wrong Mind, the way humans have been doing for centuries, we get the fear, victimhood, sin, etc.

But our true nature is of God, and the Ego cannot wholly suppress it! Every now and then, even in the "worst" people, that holiness shines through and manifests as peace, love, hope, kindness, etc. So if we practice thinking with our Right Mind more and more, beautiful, loving, peaceful things and experiences will automatically appear in our lives. They were actually always there, but the ego only points out the nasty things to you, and doesn't bother to notice the "good" stuff. So this is the Human Experiment in a nutshell.

So now let's talk about teaching methods. Let's say you want to learn to swim. A swimming teacher may just throw you off the dock into freezing cold water, and you fight for your survival. Sink or swim, you know? Or a swimming teacher can start you off in waist-high warm water on a tropical beach, supporting you from underneath while teaching you how to float, then how to use your arms and legs in the water. You can learn to swim either way, but the teacher you choose determines whether or not the experience will be a pleasant one. The Ego is the first teacher. The Holy Spirit is the second one.

You get to choose your teacher by choosing which one to listen to.

There's an old Native American story about the two wolves. The teacher tells the student that there are two wolves at war within our being: a ravenous, brutal beast, and a loving, warm companion. They are constantly at war with each other. "Which one will win?" asks the student. "The one you feed," said the teacher.[5]

So whenever you feel terrible, you're listening to the situation from Ego's point of view. You're interpreting it from perspective of the Wrong Mind, and it's only going to point out the negative parts of the story. The Ego really only wants to do something if it benefits itself, and is always asking, "What's in it for me?" But the good news is, you can *always* change your mind! Listen to the Teacher of Peace, think with your Right Mind, call on the Holy Spirit instead. Then you can look past all that sadness and discomfort, see that the "I" that is feeling terrible, is not really you! That shift in perspective changes everything!! So don't choose to help or be loving toward another because of what you'll get out of it materially. Choose love because it creates the life you really want. In fact, it's what you long for. Our entire lifetime here is spent trying to find our way in the darkness back to our Source. Your guidance system is your emotional state. Your guide along this path is The Holy Spirit, and He is within you. Always.

Happiness is what God wants for you! In fact, joy is your birthright. And it's present in you Now. Doesn't matter about your health, your looks, your wealth, how many

---
[5] Old Cherokee parable

friends you have, or anything of the world. You just need to quiet the mind and align your thinking with it to experience it. Quieting your mind means slowly eliminating thoughts of envy, comparison with others, resentment, self-pity. Let it all go. It hides your joy from you.

Hard Times

Difficult and challenging times often have a purpose, but it's hardly ever the purpose you think it is. After you come through them, you can look at others with that same compassion and empathy that you needed at the time. After all, they are caught in their own limitations and beliefs, in a bad space, listening to the Teacher of Chaos, not knowing they have a choice, and now you can relate to that with understanding, compassion, and love for them. Now you can be of use to them.

It takes practice to stay in the Now, to keep "seeing" through the Holy Spirit's eyes, ignoring the "reality" of the separation your physical eyes show you, and to go with the flow. But just keep growing your awareness! When you catch yourself feeling terrible, *change your mind.* Tell the Teacher of Chaos to take a time out, and listen to the Teacher of Peace instead. And this is how you do it: sometimes you may feel terrible for hours before you remember that you don't have to feel terrible at all! The next time it happens you'll realize it faster. And even faster the time after that. Soon, feeling bad will be a fleeting emotion, and joy will be your default. Keep practicing!

We live here in seeming separateness. But remember, God never left us. He is present in our heart, and available to us *all the time*. He gave us our emotions to guide our thoughts. If you feel peace, you're actually listening to God speak to you. It's His task to bring you closer to Him. But if you feel hatred, discord, even loneliness, you're thinking with your Ego mind, whose job it is to make you believe in this illusion of separation. It's supposed to work that way!

So this is how you find your way back to God: with your feelings, with your heart. If you feel Peace in your heart, this means you believe in Peace. People think you need to live in peaceful surroundings in order to experience peace. But lasting peace is not found in peaceful surroundings. It's not found outside of you at all! So don't look for it there. It's found in your heart, and you bring it with you wherever you go. Look for it when you go out to the woods, or to the beach, or stare up into the heavens, or go shopping, or buy a new car, or when you meet new people. Look for it there because you bring it with you. Give yourself every chance you can to listen to His voice. Little by little, it starts taking away your amnesia. And once you remember this joy, you'll never want to go back to that other teacher.

Holy Spirit, think my thoughts for me! Teach me! I want joy! I want to see and think and act and live from that higher perspective. I want Your Will and mine to be the same.

Chapter 5

Thoughts and Beliefs

If you want to experience love, you MUST think loving thoughts. There is no other way.

The Leaky Roof

Once there was a beautiful castle that had beautiful hardwood floors and expensive plush carpets, but it had a leaky roof in the main dining room. The leak kept ruining the carpet and hardwood floor beneath it. The owner of the castle hired skilled workers to replace the floor and carpet, and it was as good as new. But the rains came again and ruined the new floor as well. The leak continued to expand, and before long the parlor next to the dining room also developed a leak, and the floor in there was also being ruined. This continued happening until every room in the castle had a leaky roof. Eventually, because no one thought to repair the roof, the entire castle fell into ruin, crumbled, and fell.

The leaky roof represents your beliefs: "I am not good enough", "I am unworthy and sinful", "Other people are better than me", "I deserve to be punished for what I've done". The ruined floor represents your shattered health (and other problems). You can hire the best doctors to help you restore your health, but until you change your beliefs, your health will be ruined again and again, your problems will continue to resurface in new and more painful ways, and you will suffer. And if you leave these thoughts unchallenged and untended, they will bring down the entire house of your body.

You see, fixing or restoring your health, or finding the perfect mate, or winning the lottery is not going to help you. That's the "replacing the carpeting" part of the story. Only challenging and changing your *beliefs* will fix the problem. Those beliefs are the "leaky roof" part of the story. After that, the doctors and people and money can help you, and your restored health will stay, and your other problems will lessen. The bad health, loneliness, and poverty is a problem for you, but it's not the main issue. It's the *effect*. The *cause* is your flawed beliefs. All of us face issues like this! Because we're humans! But knowing *what* to fix first is the path to freedom.

Seeing

So how do you know what to fix? How do you find the cause? How do you know when you're just replacing the flooring for nothing, fighting a losing battle? How do you "see"?

Sometimes True seeing is really difficult *because* of what you "see with your own (physical) eyes". And I'm not saying you need to ignore what you see. I am saying that you need to know you probably don't have the whole picture. You're going to need to look at it from a higher perspective.

I read a story once, actually more like a parable, about four blind men and an elephant. One man said, the elephant is like a rope. It's just thin and kind of rough. He had hold of the elephant's tail. Another said, no, the elephant is like a huge wall—higher and wider than he could reach. He was on the elephant's flank. Yet another said, what are you talking about? The elephant is like a huge flapping wing of a bird, huge, and smooth. He had hold of the elephant's ear. And the last said, absolutely not! The elephant is like a long flexible hose. He had hold of the elephant's trunk. They spent the rest of their lives arguing and defending their point of view.[6]

The point of the story is, they each could "see with their own eyes". Their experiences were each true and right enough, but each had their own limited perspective. What we see with our physical eyes is just like that. We don't have the big picture! It's actually ridiculous, and a bit arrogant to argue our "truths", isn't it? The solution is in knowing that you don't have the whole picture. That way you don't waste your life arguing and trying to be right. Only the Holy Spirit can provide that for you.

Your "goal" is to change your beliefs. This changes your thoughts, which changes your emotions, which then changes what manifests in your world. It all starts with what you believe, especially about yourself. I would have you start by examining your beliefs about what you think you are. Perhaps you have a traumatic past, or you're suffering severe health issues. This means you believe you are a victim. I would start by examining that belief, and

---

[6] Ancient Indian parable

attempting to change it. See it differently. Change your mind. Switch teachers.

I'm guessing you're still feeling bad about yourself because you still believe in your meekness, and not in your divinity. If you think about it, God made you a glorious, beautiful, infinite entity. To insist you'd rather be meek and humble is kind of contrary to how he made you. We must embrace our holiness, our sinlessness, in order to accept his peace. Once you see yourself as holy, you'll be able to see your brothers as holy, too. That's the true definition of salvation.

There's a story in the New Testament about when some disciples had been thrown into prison. When the guards came to get them, they were singing hymns. I remember as a kid wondering how they could possibly praise God in a terrible place like that. But they had realized that one's joy is not found in their surroundings. It's found in your heart. Your current prison is your fear and your pain and your guilt. Decide to lay the thought of them aside, even just for a few minutes, and fill your heart with thoughts of peace and wellness. Focus on the *feeling*. If you want a thing, you have to Be that thing. If you want peace, you have to act peacefully. If you want joy, you need to look for it within, embrace it, become it. No matter what's going on around you. It's all about what you Believe.

So step outside of the problem, and look back at it. Notice the Ego and what it's doing, what emotion you are experiencing, and what all that is trying to make you *believe*. Our *beliefs* determine our reality. The Ego's job is to make you *believe* in separation. That's why it's here! But the bottom line is, you get to decide what to *believe*. You don't have to *believe* everything the Ego (the voice in your head) tells you. So if the Ego tells you that you're ugly, and then you feel bad, then it has succeeded in making you *believe* what it says. That *belief* becomes your own. You think that's who and what you are. You think that when it puts you down, what it's saying is true. But you can only feel bad if you *believe* it. We know better now. We know what we really are, and it's not shameful and ugly. The Ego's insults have no power over us. Remember *A Course In Miracles says*, "I am not a body. I am free. For I am still as God created me."[7] Remember how the Holy Spirit sees you: a beautiful, eternal, glorious spirit. If you are unable to see yourself this way, you won't be able to look at anyone else and see their True Self, either. This is the key to breaking our amnesia—to winning the game. "Above all else I want to see."[8]

Your beliefs determine your thoughts. Example: a man believes he was betrayed by a friend. He believes he is a victim, and his enemy now needs to pay. His thoughts will be filled by this belief with hatred and plots of revenge, and every step he takes into the future will be guided by his beliefs. He has laid the foundation for a life bent on justice. Another example: a woman believes that she is ugly and useless because her husband has told her this many times. Her thoughts are filled with despair and shame, and every time she tries to break free of him, she fails *because she believes him*. Her beliefs guide her into a future of sadness and grief. In both of the examples, the people have the option to change their mind. He can decide that he may have been mistaken and forgive his

---

[7] *A Course in Miracles* Lesson 199
[8] *A Course in Miracles* Lesson 27

friend, and she can decide not to believe her cruel husband. If they change their minds, they change their futures. Lots of things can happen to "make" us think we believe certain things. Some people believe eating meat is bad, some believe black and brown people are inferior, some believe God is jealous and punitive, etc. These beliefs fill their minds with stories that reinforce their beliefs, and these stories (thoughts) attract people and experiences into their lives that will tell the same kind of stories, reinforcing their beliefs, and they just dig a deeper and deeper hole. The harmful thoughts always come from the Ego. They come from fear. The way out is always the same: love. Choose your beliefs wisely. Does a thing you believe cause you pain? If it does, you will surely invite more pain into your life because of it. Change your mind. Replace it with loving beliefs. Doing so will bring you peace.

Is it Really Real?

One of the daily lessons in *A Course in Miracles* says, "I give meaning to all I see".[9] This idea gives you a way to understand what you *really* see around you. Example: two people are walking down a city street together. One is poor and one is wealthy. They pass a tall skyscraper. The poor man sees the skyscraper and feels inadequate, because he doesn't have the education to apply for a job up there. In his mind's eye he sees a fancy corner office with a great view up on the fortieth floor, a huge oak desk, a built-in bar, and a private secretary, and he's filled with bitterness and resentment. The wealthy man looks at the

---

[9] *A Course in Miracles* Lesson 2

same building and remembers that his father retired from an office in that very building. In his mind's eye he remembers a fancy corner office with a great view up on the fortieth floor, a built-in bar, and a huge oak desk that he used to visit from the time when he was very young. He owes his current wealth and social status to that place! He's filled with a sense of gratitude and superiority.

So the thing you see with your physical eyes is the skyscraper. But the *meaning* you assign the skyscraper is what you really "see". Every single person on the planet will "see" a different thing when they look at the same skyscraper. One may think the building is a wonderful monument to man's ingenuity. Another thinks it's an eyesore and remembers how that corner used to look before it was built. Another thinks it's a beautiful building. Another hates the color it's painted. Each reaction from each person is colored with emotion, so it's your *thoughts and beliefs* that determine what that thing is to you.

Take it a step further: can there be any truth to a thing if it becomes something different to every single person who sees it? To understand what a thing is to you, examine your emotions about it. Because the thing doesn't exist in truth, and you give it all the meaning it has for you.

Something to think about: if my example of the skyscraper blows your mind, think about what you "see" when you look into a mirror at yourself. You are giving your reflection *all* the meaning it has for you.

It's what we see *with our minds* that is different for everyone. In my skyscraper example, the building itself doesn't change, no matter who sees it. But everyone sees it differently because of their thoughts, their beliefs, past, their programming. Even if you were to have new physical eyes given to you, it wouldn't make a difference in what you see because you see with your mind, not your eyes. So how to change what you see. Can you guess? You must change your beliefs.

In the case of looking in a mirror, you see what you see for many reasons. You see what you've been told to see by society, by your parents, by magazines, by advertisements, and multiple sources of other programming. You see your past behaviors when you look in the mirror. You see every insult you've ever had thrown at you. You see what you believe your illnesses look like. Each of these judgements comes with an emotional reaction: sadness, frustration, revulsion, shame, hopelessness, etc. These emotions give what you see the power to *believe* what you see it to be, and not challenge or question it. This is exactly what the Ego is going for.

So how do you see the truth? You don't look with your eyes. You look with your heart. Truth is not found in the physical. If you stop and think about it, your body itself is not the same body that you had yesterday. It is changing continuously. Your skin and cells are constantly dying and regenerating. You literally don't have the same body from one day to the next. In fact, every cell in your body has died and been replaced several times a year. This miraculous process continues all through your life on earth, making all things new, giving you new hope for miracles every single moment. So when you do look in a mirror, don't just look with your eyes. Examine your thoughts, beliefs, and reactions. Then challenge and question those judgements. Remember who you are.

"You are not a body. You are free. For you are still as God created you."[10] Pray this *A Course in Miracles* lesson, too: "Above all else, I want to see".[11] God help me see.

Guilt

About the guilt. This is a huge step, getting rid of the guilt. So let's ask questions. Why do you still think you are guilty? Is it because you've done something "bad"? Or maybe a series of "bad" things over the years? Or is it over something "bad" you're doing now and can't stop doing? Or you think you're just a "bad" person? Or, or, or? Let's take a look at why you think (why your Ego thinks) you need to feel guilty.

First, notice that everything "bad" you've ever done is in the past. It's over, and can never come back. Anything from the past that makes you feel guilty is first in line to be let go. Let it go. I like to picture putting these "bad" things in one of those helium balloons and going outside and letting it go. Keep filling them up with each "bad" thing you think of and take them all outside. Then just watch them float away, one by one. You can even picture that you're giving them directly to God. He catches the balloons, and they totally disappear.

Second, nothing here is ever, *ever* held against you by God. There is no need for him to punish you, or hold you accountable for anything you do here on the earth. In fact, it is not in the nature of God to demand punishment or

---

[10] *A Course in Miracles* Lesson 199
[11] *A Course in Miracles* Lesson 27

payment from any of us. He is Unconditional Love. That means there *are* no conditions. He loves you no matter what. No Matter What. He *is* you! It *is* in the nature of the Ego to demand punishment, accountability, retribution, justice. People (Egos) do that. God does not.

So if you don't want to deal with the physical ramifications of doing "bad" things, then you have to make the choice to stop doing them. But it's probably not what you're actually doing right now that's causing the guilt. It's what you're thinking. You have the power to fix that. Change your mind.

Third, the best thing to do for guilt is to lighten up. Guilt is heavy, and it weighs you down. It can totally halt your progress. It's the lowest vibrational frequency on the scale. If you radiate with a vibration of guilt, you will automatically attract low frequency events and things into your life. So if you don't want more guilt in your life, you need to decide to stop feeling guilty—to let it go. There is no other way.

The Ego uses guilt to make sure it stays in charge. For instance, as long as you feel guilt, you believe you are undeserving of things "good" people have. You believe you deserve punishment, and must be punished. Remember it's your beliefs that determine what your life looks and feels like. Taking away the guilt is a huge step in taking back your power.

So here's a great meditation for you. Ask your questions: "What do I feel guilty about?" For each of your answers, imagine that big helium balloon, and place that guilt inside the balloon. Let the balloon go, let it float up to God. Imagine that when He catches the balloon, it totally disintegrates. Poof! Guilt gone. Then smile. This is an important step. Think how much lighter you feel without that burden, and smile. Then ask the question again, and repeat the process. This is a wonderful exercise in letting go. It's a wonderful exercise in lightening up.

Eventually, you'll end up arriving at a point where you just get so irritated and so sick of that feeling of guilt, shame, and helplessness. Rejoice! That point is called anger, and anger is a powerful force. You've gotten tired of taking directions from your Ego, and have said *"No more!"* That is lasting change. A powerful emotion gives you the energy you need to cut right through the guilt and helplessness. And combined with your *intention* and *willingness* to change, you do it and it is done!

Now if anger can provide you with that much power, imagine what *Love* can do!!

Chapter 6

The Bible

When you get right down to it, enlightenment, awareness, unconditional love, things like that can't be learned or studied. Because they're not things you can explain or define with your mind. They are higher states of Being that need to be experienced. There is no "understanding" them. At best, all spiritual texts are only signposts. They can point you in the right general direction, but that's the best they can do. Following them literally doesn't get you very far. You "get there" by asking for help from the Holy Spirit, practicing stillness and forgiveness, listening to your heart, serving others with love, and putting love and peace in everything you do and think. Be the change you want to see in the world.

My guideline for reading the Bible is to only take to heart the *loving* things it says. Remember God is Love and God is all and God is in all. Love is the only real thing around us. Everything you see is either an expression of love (light), or a call for love (shadow).

There are a lot of good things to say about any religious text. But they were all written by humans, and humans have forgotten the Truth. The Ego does most of the writing. Truth is hidden in there, but it's hard to see under all the thousands of years of tradition, dogma, and cultural differences. Spirit is growing. Always growing. The problem with the Bible is that it doesn't change or grow. Humans must evolve to thinking and living through the heart, not the head. I have come to realize that God and Jesus do not wish to be worshipped. They only want one thing from you: to have you accept that you are Love: the same love as they are, and join them in bliss. Remember who you are. You are not a body. You are His.

For centuries humans have used scriptures to put others down, take over entire kingdoms, enslaving whole swaths of other humans, and justify killing their neighbors, all in God's name. There's too much Ego in them to be spiritually educational. Having said that, yes there are good churches and good mosques and good synagogues, and church people out there that are loving, kind, caring servants. There is no real answer to the question of "are the churches good" because it's all very personal, individual case by case. There is really no way to tell what's in your brother's heart. My wish for you is that you don't take everything so seriously. Remember, there is only love. Love does not judge or condemn. There is no punishment, no eternal damnation for "wrongdoers". The Ego wants judgement and payback. God does not.

Chapter 7

Attitude

There's another big thing that is influenced by your beliefs, and that's attitude. For instance, if you believe you're a broken, ruined person, your attitude will be "why bother" most of the time. If you believe you're a radiant, eternal being, your attitude will be more like "what wonderful thing can I do for you today?" Can you see how the actual "flavor" of your day is determined by this?

So stop saying "I can't" and start saying "I can". Focus on what you can do and what you do have, instead of what you can't do, and what you don't have. A little gratitude goes a long way. And everyone has something to be grateful for. Sometimes you have to hunt a little for it, granted! But excuses aren't helping you. They're actually holding you back.

Look up more, and down less. Smile more than you frown. And forgive yourself at all times! You have been programed to think the way you think, but you are not limited to your programing! You can escape from it! You already have. Breathe and be at peace. Always ask the Holy Spirit to help you see all the radiance in plain sight all around you.

Most of us search for joy, peace, and happiness, but we think that we can find it in "things": a thinner, healthier body, a more beautiful face, a sure path. It reminds me of the story of the man who lost his car keys. He's searching his front lawn over and over and over, looking for those keys. A neighbor comes by and asks him what he's looking for, and he says, "I've lost my car keys, and I just can't find them!" So the neighbor helps him look, and together they search the front yard thoroughly, but they still can't find the keys. So the neighbor says, "Well, where did you last see them?" And he thought a minute and said, "I had them last time I changed my clothes." The neighbor was confused then, and said, "Did you change your clothes out here on the front lawn? Why are we looking out here?" And the man said, "No, I changed them inside. But the light is better for searching out here." So search all you want! But if your attitude is in the wrong place, you won't find anything.

Know that you are beautiful right now! That's true seeing. But it doesn't mean you can't "work on yourself". Do yourself a favor and choose to be kind to yourself. Nothing gives your attitude a boost like being kind. Many of us are kind-hearted to others, but we insist on criticizing ourselves mercilessly. Ego is really very good at that!

So make those little or large changes for your own comfort and well-being. The motivation to do so does not have to come out of a place of dissatisfaction. Making changes with a joyful heart makes the process an awesome, enjoyable experience. So keep "wanting" to "get better". Keep improving yourself, your conditions, your life. It's a way of setting your intention, and it keeps you pointed in the right direction. The best thing for you to remember is, don't make a change because of guilt or shame. Make a change for the joy of it. Remember that enlightenment does not mean you will have perfect physical health and no more obstacles. It means that you have learned to react to your health issues and road blocks with a joyful acceptance, making patient, inspired changes, and choosing your path with Love.

Do something nice for yourself. Doesn't have to be anything big. Maybe pick a wildflower and put it in a glass of water on your table or window sill. Maybe wash your face or take a shower, or do your hair. Maybe eat an apple or something healthy. Maybe clean out a drawer in the kitchen. Could be anything. But doing something loving from a place of calm will reinforce how lovely peace of mind is!

Keep focusing on the things that are going right. If your back hurts, focus on your legs. If your checkbook is a little skinny, focus on the hundreds of bills that have already been paid. If a relationship ends, focus on the opportunities you have with more freedom. Treat yourself with love *because you deserve it*. Kindness is the most healing thing I know of! Meditate often on your gifts and advantages. Be in a state of thanks as often as you can. Flood your Self with thoughts of kindness and peace. This is the true path to everything you ever wanted. Because what you really want is what everyone wants: happiness. You may think only a healed body, or a new lover, or a big dollar windfall will make you happy. But your happiness is already present. In your heart. Choose happiness. You do that by choosing your beliefs now. If you choose to find happiness in some future event (like getting healthy someday) you'll have to wait until that someday to be happy. If you choose right now to think thoughts of gratitude and peace and joy, you take yourself directly, *immediately* to your happiness. Be aware that you can't choose loving thoughts toward yourself or others if you hate yourself.

Health

Health is a state of Being, not a physical condition.

There is a place inside you that never gets sick, never grows sorrowful. A place of love, peace, and bliss. You carry it with you in your heart, *no matter your physical condition*. Go there as often as you can. Align your thoughts with the way God thinks, and you've arrived. There your health is permanently perfect. It's your birthright. Healing the physical body is as temporary as the body is. Fill your heart with gratitude over what you have, and don't give what you don't have a second thought. This is how you manifest wellness and peace.

Longing, wishing for good health is not going to get you very far. In fact, it may hinder the return of good health to your body. You see, all illness comes from fear. It's a product of the Ego's paranoia and its belief that danger is everywhere. It believes its safety is the most important thing in the universe, and if it's not in immediate danger, it will manifest illness. Just to prove it was right to worry. It's all about your fear level. So ask yourself, "How afraid of wellness am I?" Or maybe for you it's, "How undeserving of perfect health am I?"

Then change your mind! Listen to the Teacher of Peace instead. He will undo the paranoia, fear, and loneliness, because He simply doesn't see it. His vision is only the

Real. He sees you for what you are in Truth. This is your goal: to see as He sees.

"BROKEN"

(Author ~ John Roedel)

Me: Hey God.

God: Hello, my love.

Me: I'm falling apart. Can you put me back together?

God: I would rather not.

Me: Why?

God: Because you aren't a puzzle.

Me: What about all of the pieces of my life that are falling down onto the ground?

God: Let them stay there for a while. They fell off for a reason. Take some time and decide if you need any of those pieces back.

Me: You don't understand! I'm breaking down!

God: No - you don't understand. You are breaking through. What you are feeling are just growing pains. You are shedding the things and the people in your life that are holding you back. You aren't falling apart. You are falling into place. Relax. Take some deep breaths and allow those things you don't need any more to fall off of you. Quit holding onto the pieces that don't fit you anymore. Let them fall off. Let them go.

Me: Once I start doing that, what will be left of me?

God: Only the very best pieces of you.

Me: I'm scared of changing.

God: I keep telling you – You aren't changing!! You're becoming!!

Me: Becoming who?

God: Becoming who I created you to be: a person of light and love and charity and hope and courage and joy and mercy and grace and compassion. I made you for more than the shallow pieces you have decided to adorn yourself with that you cling to with such greed and fear. Let those things fall off of you. I love you! Don't change! Become! Become! Become! Become who I made you to be. I'm going to keep telling you this until you remember it.

Me: There goes another piece.

God: Yep. Let it be.

Me: So...I'm not broken?

God: No - but you are breaking like the dawn. It's a new day. Become!! Become!! [12]

---

[12] Author John Roedel. Used with permission.

Good and Bad

Once there was a man who lived on a farm with a grown son. One day the son went far out into the mountains and came home with a beautiful wild horse. All the man's neighbors came over to see the horse and they said, "What a beautiful horse! This is such a good thing that has happened to you!" And the man said, "Perhaps." The next day, the son was working with the horse, trying to break him so that he could be used to ride the long road into the nearest town, and the son was thrown from the horse and he broke his leg. He was in great pain. All the man's neighbors came by to help and they said, "What a bad thing that has happened here!" And the man said, "Perhaps." The next day some army officials came by the farm to draft young men into the army to go away to war. But the man was too old to go, and the son had a broken leg, so neither of them had to go away to war. And all the neighbors came by to rejoice with them, and they said, " What a good thing has happened for you! Such good fortune!" And the man said, "Perhaps."[13]

The point of the story is, we never actually know if something that happens is a "good" thing or a "bad" thing, and there's no sense labeling them "good" or "bad". Right now you think your bad health is a "bad" thing because it is so uncomfortable. But it may be like the broken leg in our story. Yes, it's painful, but it's better than what would have happened if the leg had *not* been broken. I know how important it seems that you recover, and recover fast. But you need to let go of that. I don't mean stop trying! I mean

---

[13] Ancient Chinese fable

let go of the outcome. True healing is of the mind and heart—not the body. Get your mind on *feeling* better, not *getting* better.

Practical Advice

Most spiritual books like this one are full of spiritual advice, like the kind you've been reading about so far. But bad health can provide the kind of tangible "proof" that the Ego keeps warning you about: physical pain, poor digestion, bad skin, hair loss, etc. These things can sap all of your attention, making it extremely difficult to focus on all these spiritual ideals. All that stuff goes right out the window when you're dealing with surgery, or chemotherapy, or suffering with great physical or mental anguish. So as a health coach, I'm going to give you a whole section on what you can do to help improve your immediate physical condition. It's called NEWS, which stands for Nutrition, Exercise, Water, and Sleep (Stress management). (Note: this is not a substitution for a regime of medication and medicine to manage extreme pain. If you can't stand the pain, this is the twenty-first century! For goodness sake, get some medical help!)

Nutrition is really important. Here in the United States we have what I call the SAD (Standard American Diet). Too many processed foods. Too much sugar. Too many things that aren't food at all: artificial colors and flavors, preservatives, pesticides, and antibiotics. I will grant you that for many people, y'all can eat as much of that junk as you want and you never gain a pound. Whatever symptoms you develop can be explained away or otherwise justified—anything so you can eat whatever and whenever you want. That's fine if you're currently in great health. Any serious health concerns may be decades away for you if you go on eating as you want. But if you're currently very ill, make these changes:

    A.   Stop eating processed foods. Anything that comes in a box has been processed so that it can remain in the box without spoiling, and if you check the label, you're sure to find lots of sugar, artificial colors and flavors, and preservatives. Rule of thumb: if you can't pronounce it, don't eat it. It's not food. Change up that bowl of cereal for fresh fruit and cottage cheese. And don't go anywhere near those whole-meal-in-a-box things.

    B.   Eat more whole, raw, organic fruits and vegetables. I know, lots of people will remind you that organic farmers spray their fields with pesticides, too. But organic pesticides are water soluble, and easy to get off the food, and they don't contain known carcinogens. And organic foods have not been genetically modified with the DNA of animals or the molecular structure of harmful chemicals. That's not food, either.

    C.   Supplements may or may not help you, depending on how the vitamins were extracted from foods, how free of toxins they are, and how you combine them. At the least, they'll just give you really expensive urine. At the worst, they can be harmful to your health. Look for organic supplements certified toxin-free by the NSF. And double check with a nutritionist, not a doctor. Doctors don't know jack about nutrition.

D. Get some exercise. They say that sitting is the new cancer. American society in particular has sit down jobs, sit down television, sit down computer games, sit down everything. Moving is necessary for your lymphatic system, as it doesn't have a circulatory pump like blood does. Moderate exercise like walking, swimming, or biking (not jogging or running) can improve your overall health immensely! Twenty minutes three times a week. Find some easy exercise videos on the internet and do them. Take the stairs. Take your bicycle.

E. Drink lots and lots of water. Drink enough water so that your urine runs clear. Every day. I know it's a pain, because you have to pee all the time. But do you want to help your health or make it worse? Water (not coffee, tea, soda, or juice) is nature's cleansing tool. All your body's systems work better when you're properly hydrated. After all, your body is made of mostly water.

F. Sleep eight hours a night. Sleep is the most restorative elixir I've ever heard about—just plain undrugged sleep. Illness may cause insomnia, and if this is the case, bedtime rituals can help a lot. For example, go to bed. Don't sleep in your chair one night, couch the next, chair the next. Before bed is important, too. No electronic devices for at least an hour before you turn in. They keep your mind very busy, and it's harder to shut down and sleep.

No food for at least three hours before bed. Digesting is one of the most difficult tasks your body accomplishes every day. Moving around helps this process—not sleep. Wash your face, brush your teeth, and put on pajamas and get comfortable. Make sure your bed is comfortable in the extreme. This means lots of heavy comforters, soft pillows, and sheets. Get some ear buds or one of those headband type head phones and meditate as you fall asleep. Pick out a video that has rain sounds, or forest sounds, or wave sounds, or any kind of healing sounds. Just make sure your device is upside down so there's no light coming from it. And turn off any sounds it makes. Darken your bedroom. Your body craves sleep when you're ill. Give this to yourself.

G. Meditate or go to therapy or talk to a friend, or get some help, or do whatever it takes to keep your stress level down. I know you're used to multi-tasking, working two jobs and taking care of the kids and the pets and the house. That's also fine if you're currently in good health. But if you're ill, overwork and stress will only make things worse.

Addiction and Meditation

It's the middle of the night, you're awake, you're restless, you get the urge to indulge your addiction. Maybe let's try a distraction: go to your closet and move all the clothes around. Put all the tops and shirts together in a row. Hang up all your pants and put them together by color. Just don't do that addiction thing. While you're playing in the closet, ask your Ego the question: is there a Reason you want me to smoke (eat, drink, take drugs)? What is the Reason? Where did you ever get the idea that doing that right now would be a good idea? Then listen to the voice in your head. I'm guessing it will start giving you excuses, then start putting you down and bullying you when those excuses don't work on you. When this happens, stop and put your hand up like you're telling an imaginary person to *stop* right there. Smile at this imaginary Ego person and kindly say, no, thank you. I've decided to go back to bed instead.

Then, as you're lying there trying to go back to sleep, meditate on your breath. Inhale to a count of six, and exhale to a count of eight. Inhale the good vibrations, exhale the bad vibrations. Notice what that feels like. Listen to your heart calm down and beat regularly, rhythmically. Marvel at the work it does to keep you alive. Close your eyes whenever you want, and notice how nice it feels just to lay down and close your eyes. Notice how comfortable your bed and pillow are. Give thanks for having a warm, dry, comfortable place to sleep. Give thanks for your breath and your heartbeat. And just breathe.

Caring

You still believe that time will heal your body and "everything will be alright again, so don't worry too much about it, and do the best you can." This hopeful attitude has some merit, but it's also holding you back from making a full recovery. "Everything will be alright again" is an outcome that you hope for. Let go of the outcome. Time, discipline, and hard work do have their benefits, but the truth is there is no guarantee that you will ever be as healed as the Ego wishes. That's kind of a bottomless pit. Nothing is ever good enough for it.

So don't eat right and take special care of yourself because you're working toward some ideal image of a beautiful, healed body. Eat right because you care so incredibly much about yourself that you can't *wait* to do something kind for yourself! And when you look into the mirror, you'll see that kindness.

Chapter 8

Fear

How I describe fear came to me after reading an *A Course in Miracles* daily lesson concerning what it called "attack thoughts".[14] It was all about how fearful thinking can determine your life course, and how to break that cycle. What follows is my "parable" that helped me understand fear:

I see in my mind a frightened, abandoned cat, and a kind woman who is trying to take it home and love it. When she reaches out to the cat to help it, it feels nothing but fear, because that's all it has ever known. The cat hisses and attacks, trying to scratch and bite her, and the woman is prevented from helping it. But every day the woman comes back and brings it a treat and tries to talk with it. And every day the fear is a little bit less, until finally the cat allows the woman to pick it up and take it home with her.

The cat is you, and the woman in the story is God. When you feel fear, you actually are cutting off the very help you need for your salvation, and you're doing it with your own attack thoughts. But God is very patient, and keeps offering you more and more opportunities to overcome your fear, until you are ready to accept His help. He will never force His way in, because this would cause you even more fear. He is always willing to care for you, but you *must* be willing to accept His help. This always means

---

[14] *A Course in Miracles* Lesson 23

letting go of your fear. Always. You do this by ignoring the Ego and giving your fear to the Holy Spirit. Then sit back and wait to see what wonders will manifest in your life.

Fear seems addicting because it's Ego driven. Ego likes you scared because you're easier to control. And Ego doesn't like change. It wants you scared all the time. Everything the Ego does is a lie, because it operates on the premise that you are separate from God, which is impossible. Some say "lie", some say "illusion", some say "mistake". No matter what you call it, there is never any need for fear unless you're being physically threatened. Then fear is your ally. It helps you with a boost of adrenaline, it's the fight or flight response there to keep your body safe. But the fear that plagues most of us chronically is not usually from being in physical danger. It is all in your mind. This is the destructive, addicting kind of fear that is simply useless, except to control your mind. That's what the Ego uses it for. The power of your presence is true because it's *real*. It's the only real thing in this world of illusion and Ego. How do you know it's real? Because it's eternal. "Now" is eternal. There will never *not* be a "Now". Everything in the world is perishable. Even the mountains are only temporary. But Now is where time and eternity intersect. That's why it's true, and why it's so powerful.

It takes a special kind of motivation and willingness to want to really know God, remember the truth about who you are, and move into a higher vibrational state of being (Bliss). The world is so very convincingly real, and it's really hard to deny it! But your happiness depends on you really wanting to learn how to see past all that, see through the trick, lift the veil, remember. The kingdom of God is truly "within you". And it's yours *now*. And it's always *now*.

Acknowledgements

Special thanks to my family and friends who helped me make this book a reality. And special thanks to my mentors online and in books whose videos and writings have influenced me the most:

Beth Geer

Rupert Spira

Eckhart Tolle

Erin Michelle Galito

Anna Brown

Gina Lake

Abraham Hicks

Alan Watts

About the Author

Kristine Stout is an artist and retired musician who resides in Rogers City, Michigan with her husband of twenty-six years, Kirt. She enjoys all kinds of creative endeavors including gardening, painting, various arts and crafts, knitting, crocheting, tatting, needlework, as well as word and number games. Between boating, swimming, beach-walking, and fishing on beautiful Lake Huron and her creative pursuits and studies, she leads a very full, active, and happy life. But her main focus now is on her spiritual studies and Life Coaching activities, which have shown her the way to true, lasting joy and peace, which she is driven to share with others.

Kristine offers free Life Coaching! Get in touch with her today.

Join Kristine's Facebook Group, at
Facebook.com/groups/CanYouPleaseExplainThat

Visit her website at
www.CanYouPleaseExplainThat.com

Email her at CanYouPleaseExplainThat@Gmail.com

www.ingramcontent.com/pod-product-compliance
Lightning Source LLC
Chambersburg PA
CBHW022341040426
42449CB00026B/627